The Assessment Playbook

A UDL Approach

A Companion to the Universal Design for Learning (UDL) Assessment Video Series

Edited by Amanda Bastoni and Allison Posey

CAST | Until learning has no limits·

Paperback ISBN 978 1 930583 77 1
Ebook ISBN 978 1 930583 78 8
PDF ISBN 978 1 930583 79 5

Published by:
CAST Professional Publishing
an imprint of CAST, Inc.
Wakefield, Massachusetts, USA

Cover and interior design by Happenstance Type O Rama

Bulk discounts available: For details, email **publishing@cast.org** or
visit **www.castpublishing.org**.

Table of Contents

Section 2:

Acknowledgments

We thank the <u>New Hampshire Department of Education</u>, which provided funding for the first version of this project.

Contributors include but are not limited to Amanda Bastoni, Jess Gropen, Tracey E. Hall, Allison Posey, Susan Shapiro, and Bill Wilmot.

<u>Jim Galdos</u> produced the videos and contributed much to the content and presentation, as did Mindy Johnson, Cassandra Sell, David Gordon, and Linda Gerstle at CAST. More information on the project can be found at <u>CAST: A UDL Perspective on Assessment</u> (see **https://tinyurl.com/CASTassessments**).

Welcome

The vision of this playbook is to highlight key ideas and deepen opportunities to learn more about the topics presented in the UDL assessment video series, available on CAST's YouTube channel. (See **https://tinyurl .com/CASTyouTube**.)

- Intro to Assessments
- Evaluating Assessments
- Grade Level K–2 Video
- Grade Level 3–5 Video
- Grade Level 6–8 Video
- Grade Level 9–12 Video

We hope this playbook will support K–12 educators as they plan and implement assessments that inform the design of instruction. Effective design and implementation of assessments help ensure that students can grow and develop as learners so they are empowered to build on their strengths and improve on areas of challenge.

Purpose and Audience

We developed this series at the height of the COVID-19 lockdown when assessment of student learning had to shift overnight. Instead of having face-to-face interactions with students, in which educators could see firsthand how students were progressing, instruction and assessment went fully online. This created a new set of challenges for educators, especially related to assessing student learning. However, the goals educators had for assessments remained the same: to make sure that the learning experiences they designed were relevant, meaningful, and challenging so they could meet the learning needs of every one of our students.

Our goal with this video series is to support educators to think about assessment from a Universal Design for Learning (UDL) perspective. A UDL approach to assessment includes proactive design to make sure that assessments are accessible, flexible, engaging, and aligned to the intended learning objectives. In a UDL approach to assessment, the focus is on using frequent, formative assessment to improve instruction for all students by reducing barriers that may prevent robust learning. Whereas traditional tests and diagnostics tend to focus on identifying weaknesses and disabilities in the individual learner, assessments made with a UDL approach focus more on identifying weaknesses and barriers in the design of the learning context itself. This makes it possible to probe whether a different set of options, a different path, or a different design might lead students to deeper and more meaningful learning and opportunities to express what they know or can do.

Educators, parents, administrators, assessment designers/developers, and students themselves all need accurate assessments and timely results from these assessments to use as feedback to inform the next steps in the instructional design of the goals, methods, and materials. Formative assessments are designed to be part of an ongoing feedback loop that can be used to understand what students know and can do—and to identify what they need to deepen their learning or skill development. Instructional approaches with a foundation in UDL incorporate formative assessments to help reduce the inadvertent barriers to learning that many students face, making the assessment of learning progress more accurate, informative, and useful, and they enable all learners to become masters of learning itself. A UDL approach to assessment assumes and anticipates variability among all learners and asserts that when we apply the UDL framework to assessment design, more learners will benefit, providing teachers with better evidence to make instructional decisions.

In addition, a UDL approach incorporates recurring and flexible assessments throughout instruction to provide ongoing, actionable feedback that educators and students can use before failure takes place and when taking action can make a real difference for all. When we use flexible, formative assessments, we gather multiple sources of data that can help us better understand what students need to succeed in their learning. Such formative assessments also enable educators to provide mastery-oriented feedback to students so they are able to continue to make progress in their learning—and so they can become masters of learning itself.

Finally, a UDL approach ensures fundamental access to assessments. The UDL Guidelines (**https://udlguidelines .cast.org**) highlight ways to design assessments that ensure that learners can (a) perceive and make meaning of the content, (b) express and communicate what they know or can do, and (c) engage, persist, and self-regulate during the assessment. To learn more about how to make your assessments accessible, visit the <u>National Center on Accessible Materials (AEM Center)</u> at **https://aem.cast.org** to explore free videos and resources. There, you will learn how to ensure your assessments are perceivable, operable, understandable, and robust (POUR), a framework designed by the Web Accessibility Initiative.

The videos produced in this series build upon educators' current assessment practices and illustrate specific strategies for designing assessments using the <u>UDL Guidelines</u>. However, no prerequisite knowledge of UDL is required—these videos will help any educator wanting to reflect upon or improve their assessment practice. We hope this playbook supports your assessment design to ensure all students gain the knowledge, skills, and background to become successful, lifelong learners—until learning has no limits, as we like to say at CAST.

How to Use This Guide

In this guide, there are two main sections. The first section contains an overview of the key ideas from the video content, links to transcripts, and guiding questions. The second section contains resources you can consult to learn more, including resources on UDL, assessments, accessibility, and communicating with parents and caregivers. Please use the videos and resources flexibly. For example, you could

- Watch the videos on your own, with a colleague, or with a professional learning community. Or you could watch the videos on your own and then come together as a small group or team to discuss the ideas that resonated or the actions you will take in your practice.

- Watch the videos at your own pace so you can pause, rewind, or fast forward to parts of need or interest. Share the videos with colleagues you think might be interested.

- Self-reflect on your practice using the discussion prompts, which are found within the videos and in this playbook. Brainstorm action steps you can take to make small but effective changes to your assessments. Observe changes in student engagement and learning as a result of your assessment design.

- Use the discussion questions as prompts for conversations with your colleagues, parents and caregivers, and/or administrators in your school or professional learning community. Include students in the discussion and design of assessments that help them best show what they know and can do.

- Use the resources in this playbook to deepen your understanding or learning on any of the topics covered here. We have also collected them online at **https://tinyurl.com/CASTpubAssess**.

Section 1

Video Summaries and Discussion Questions

These are the six videos:

- An introductory video has been designed to help you understand the different kinds of assessments used in classrooms, common barriers in assessments, and key strategies for developing assessments for students.

- The Evaluating Assessments video has specific strategies for approaching the design of any assessment in any content area or grade. It includes specific language that helps identify the central construct of an assessment, potential barriers to completing the assessment, and tips for including flexibility in the assessment.

- Grade-specific videos: K–2, 3–5, 6–8, 9–12. Each grade-specific video has general recommendations, suggestions, tips, and resources that relate to assessments for the specific age group. These videos are important for understanding some of the unique challenges and opportunities at the different grade levels. Videos also include examples of different ideas for assessment at each grade level.

Intro to Assessments

Welcome and Introduction

"Intro to Assessments" video (See **https://tinyurl .com/CASTvideoIntro**.)

The purpose of the introductory video is to encourage educators to reflect on why assessments are important, whether they might be improved, and what barriers or challenges teachers face in creating and using assessments. We discuss some of the challenges educators face in remote and online learning, including understanding what students have learned during remote learning and where there may be gaps in the learning that need to be addressed. Such considerations will help educators plan their instruction.

In this video, *assessments* are defined as the techniques we use to find the information we need to understand what happened and what we can do to help, and this video recognizes that teachers already do much of this. Assessments help reveal where students are, and where teachers and learners together need to go next. We discuss strategies for how to use assessments, especially formative assessments that focus on each student as an individual.

Formative Assessments

Key ideas

- *Formative assessments* are short and help educators determine where there may be gaps in student learning. *Summative assessments* are large end-of-unit measures.

- Examples of formative assessments include those that pose questions in class about the content, questions about the emotional state of the student, and questions in exit tickets, items evidenced in student work, and feedback or interactions between educators and students.

- Look for ways in which your assessments can connect to real-world skills and situations to increase engagement in assessments.

Discussion questions

- In your own words, define *formative* and *summative assessments* (hint: think about the GPS analogy). How do you plan to integrate formative assessments this year?

  Sentence starters:

  - Formative assessments are different from summative assessments because . . .

  - This year, I plan to use formative assessments such as . . .

- How do you design opportunities in your assessments that students can use to make personal connections?

  Sentence starter:

  - In my assessments, I encourage students to make personal connections by . . .

Have more time or want to learn more?

- What role will formative assessments play in your return-to-school strategy?

- How do you use data gathered by formative assessments to inform your instruction?

What Gets in the Way?

Key ideas

- Be aware that concerns about students returning to school with gaps—such as achievement, opportunity, or "learning loss"—can lead to a deficit approach to teaching and learning.

- We can use assessment to find out where kids are and how they learn best so that we can design to support their learning.

- We can identify and reduce *barriers*, or roadblocks, that prevent students from achieving a learning goal. Barriers can include learners' variable background knowledge, instructions that are presented in only one way, and social/emotional demands. Sometimes barriers are built into the design of the assessments.

- Remember that barriers reside in the design of the environment—not in students themselves.

- Teachers also can face barriers in terms of assessments, but we can expand our notion of assessments so they become anything that helps us gather information about student learning.

- Assessment is not about what has not been accomplished; instead it is something we can share and discuss with students.

Discussion questions

- What barriers have you seen students experience in your classroom related to their learning or in their assessments?

  Sentence starter:

  - I noted my students experience barriers to learning when . . .

- As you develop assessments, ask yourself, "What barriers might be present for students in this assessment?" How would you answer this question about an upcoming assessment?

Sentence starters:

- Barriers my students may face in my assessment include . . .

- I know this because . . .

Have more time or want to learn more?

- How do you think the quote Allison shared—"When a flower doesn't bloom, you fix the environment in which it grows, not the flower"—relates to education?

- How is removing barriers different from removing the challenging aspects of a lesson, task, or assignment?

- When was a time in which you experienced barriers in your own learning?

- Watch "Disabling Segregation," a TEDx Talk by Dan Habib (~18 minutes; see **https://tinyurl.com /HabibVideo**). Why is it important to make sure all students are included and have access to *all* aspects of learning—including demonstrating what they know?

Seven Tips for Good Assessments

Key ideas

- To analyze any assessment, ask the following questions:
    - How is the assessment linked to the learning goal?
    - How does the assessment engage the learner?
    - What barriers might students experience?

- Reflect on the seven tips for good assessments:
    1. Align the assessment with the learning goal.
    2. Provide multiple ways in which students can show what they know. You can have high expectations, but include flexible means in your assessments.
    3. Examine how well students can transfer learning to meaningful situations.
    4. Look for barriers.
    5. Empower students to learn how they learn.
    6. Look for informal assessment opportunities including engaging parents and caregivers in the conversation about their student's learning.
    7. Provide frequent, timely doses of feedback.
- Mastery-oriented feedback is timely and targeted and is specific to the task at hand. It also encourages persistence and suggests next steps.

Discussion questions

- What strategies do you use to make sure assessments connect to the learning goal?

    Sentence starter:
    - To make sure assessments connect to the learning goal, I . . .

- Share your three favorite formative assessments. Why do you think they work well?

    Sentence starter:
    - A formative assessment I use is . . . This works well because . . .

Have more time or want to learn more?

- What resonated with you about the GPS example from the video?

- What are some of the ways in which you provide mastery-oriented feedback to students? What strategies can you share with a colleague?

- Analyze one of your assessments with any of the seven tips for good assessments. What is one way in which you can improve one of your assessments?

- Watch the TEDx Talk from skateboarder Dr. Tae, "Can Skateboarding Save Our Schools?" (~14 minutes; see **https://tinyurl.com/SkateboardEducation**).

- Share one idea for redesigning an assessment that would make it feel more relevant and/or might make it more useful for students.

Assessment Examples

Key ideas

- **Example #1:** Use formative assessments to understand students' emotional states.

- **Example #2:** The stoplight strategy can be used to ask students to share something they learned (green light), something they have a question about (yellow light), or something that stopped their learning (red light).

- **Example #3:** Enhanced exit tickets can include questions about content, emotional states during learning, resources that were used, or barriers that students faced.

- **Example #4:** Mastery-oriented feedback can be given that is specific to the task, that encourages students to persist, and that suggests next steps.

Discussion questions

- Why are assessments important—especially now?

  Sentence starter:

  - After watching this video, my perspective on assessments has . . .

- How do you plan to communicate about assessments with students and parents?

  Sentence starter:

  - Ways I plan to communicate about assessments with students and parents include . . .

Have more time or want to learn more?

- Watch Carol Dweck's TED Talk, "The Power of Believing That You Can Improve" (~10 minutes; **https://tinyurl.com/CDweckTED**). What aspects of a growth mindset can you apply to teaching this year? How can you share this message with your students?

- Check out the full list of resources at the end of the playbook, including strategies for connecting with parents and families.

Conclusion

Key ideas

- Assessments provide key information we need to make sure students are moving forward with learning.

- Now is the time for gathering formative feedback quickly and accurately.

- Barriers exist in the learning environment, not in the learner. Look carefully at your assessments to make sure they are related to the learning goal, are engaging, and are flexible.

Discussion questions

- How will you gather formative feedback at the start of this school year?

- What are the next steps you will take to evaluate your assessments?

Evaluating Assessments

Welcome and Introduction

"Evaluating Assessments" video (See **https://tinyurl .com/CASTvideoEvaluating**.)

The purpose of the "Evaluating Assessments" video is to empower educators to understand how assessments are designed and some of the fundamental components of assessments. The goal is to help educators develop strategies to effectively evaluate assessments to ensure they are accurately measuring the intended learning goal and what students really know and can do.

Key ideas

- If we understand the mechanics of assessments, we can better evaluate when an assessment is working, when it is not, and where the breakdowns happen.

- We use assessments to recognize where kids are, how they learn best, and what we can design to support their learning.

- Evaluate assessments:

    ○ Understand the *construct*, or the knowledge, skills, or abilities, being measured by an assessment item.

    ○ Acknowledge that often, the methods or materials used in an assessment require additional skills or understanding not directly connected to what is being measured or tested. These are construct-irrelevant features that create barriers for some students so we do not get an accurate measurement of the construct.

- Educators can use formative assessment by observing students—and this can inform the decision-making process and design of the assessments (as shared in the spelling test example in the video).

- When we build assessments that focus on the construct, we understand the students' abilities more clearly—and we isolate variables.

Discussion questions

- Define *construct* and *construct irrelevant* in your own words.

  Sentence starters:
  - The construct is . . .
  - Something that is construct irrelevant is . . .

- How does using specific terminology about assessments increase your understanding and design of your assessments?

  Sentence starter:
  - Using specific terminology about assessments helps me . . .

Have more time or want to learn more?

- How do you align your assessments, materials, and methods with the construct of your lessons (as Tracey outlined in the spelling test example in the video)?

- Here is an example of an assessment item to critique based on the potential construct-irrelevant features you notice. *Imagine you are giving a timed, paper-and-pencil math assessment. The students need to solve a series of five word problems to show that they understand how to add fractions.*

- Start small! Pick a specific assessment you can work through to analyze the construct and how it aligns with your assessment.

- An image was shared and discussed in this video. What resonated with you as you learned about the image? What will you share with a colleague?

Steps for Evaluating Assessments

Key ideas

- Break down assessment items using the following steps to identify barriers in the individual questions or items (see Figure 1). Look for items that are ambiguous, misleading, or that may be construct irrelevant, preventing us from understanding what students really know.

  1. Present information: Student is presented with an item in the assessment.

  2. Interact with the construct: Student engages with the assessment item, comprehends it, and prepares to act.

  3. Produce response: Student answers the question.

  4. Quantitative score: Educators evaluate or judge the student response.

  5. Inference to construct: A barrier in any of the steps (1 through 4) can interfere with the accuracy of the assessment.

- Our job as educators is to break down the assessment so we can see the component parts, analyze what information we are really gaining, and make sure this information is really connected to the learning goal.

Figure 1. Steps for evaluating assessment

Discussion questions

- How has this video affected the way you think about barriers to learning?

    Sentence starter:

    - I had not thought about . . . as being a barrier to learning.

- What barriers do students face when engaging with assessments or when demonstrating what they know on assessments?

    Sentence starter:

    - A barrier that prevents students from engaging with or showing what they really know on an upcoming assessment is . . .

Have more time or want to learn more?

- What barriers do students face when they are building an understanding about how to take different kinds of assessments in your class?

- What supports exist in your school that you can leverage to support students who might be facing more serious barriers to learning?

- Start small! Pick a specific assessment you can go through and analyze to determine the barriers (look for construct-irrelevant features) your students may face in it. Be sure to identify whether the barrier is part of the construct.

- Consider the article "How to Break Down Barriers to Learning with UDL" by CAST's Allison Posey. See **https://tinyurl.com/BreakBarriersLD**.

Conclusion

Key ideas

- We can make more informed decisions about teaching if we analyze how and what we ask of students.

- We can talk with students about barriers they face in the assessment process so they deepen their understanding about their own learning and what they need to work on.

- By gathering and using information about student learning, we can help all of our learners reach high expectations.

Discussion questions

- This is a lot of information. What is one big takeaway you can apply from this video?

  Sentence starter:

  ○ A takeaway that resonates for me is . . .

- How can you use something you have learned about from this video to support a student in your classroom?

  Sentence starter:

  ○ To support a student in my classroom, I will . . .

Have more time or want to learn more?

- How can you teach your students about assessment design and ask them to help you design lessons?

- What is one thing from this video that you can share with a colleague?

- How do you align your assessments, materials, and methods to the construct of your lessons?

- Don't be afraid to try something new in your teaching—even if it does not work as you had hoped, think of it as part of the learning process.

- Recognize how the small steps you are taking have an impact on student learning and engagement. Share the small successes with colleagues, parents, and students.

Resources for the Evaluating Assessments Video

- A video that explains the definition of construct and construct irrelevant is at **https://tinyurl.com /CASTconstruct**.

- Lorrie Shepard's article "The Role of Assessment in a Learning Culture" on why assessment matters is at **https://www.jstor.org/stable/1176145?seq=1**.

- See this research paper on considerations for designing accessible educational scenario-based assessments for multiple populations with a focus on linguistic complexity at **https://tinyurl.com /OliveriFrontier**.

- Another paper, "The Expanded Evidence-Centered Design (e-ECD) for Learning and Assessment Systems: A Framework for Incorporating Learning Goals and Processes Within Assessment Design," is available at **https://tinyurl.com/ArieliAttali**.

- Learning modules from the Center for Assessment Classroom Assessment are available at **https:// tinyurl.com/NCIEAassessment**.

Check out the full list of resources at the end of the playbook, including strategies for connecting with parents and families.

About the Grade-Specific Videos

For each grade-level video, remember to focus attention on the three big guiding questions:

- How is the assessment linked to the learning goal?

- How does the assessment engage the learner?

- What barriers might students experience?

Assessments for Grades K–2

Welcome and Introduction

"Assessments for Grades K–2" video (See **https:// tinyurl.com/CASTvideoK2**.)

In K–2, students are just getting acclimated to school— learning the routines and foundational skills such as reading and writing, working together, and self-regulation. In this video, we share specific barriers related to this age group, general recommendations, and tips and strategies.

Key ideas

- In grades K–2, the focus is on students learning the classroom routines and how to read.

- Students bring a wide range of backgrounds and experiences to school for the first time.

- Teachers: You've got this! Look for ways to collaborate; be proud of the work of our profession. Think how you can learn about your students and their personalities, backgrounds, interests, and goals.

Discussion questions

- What are some specific barriers to learning facing students in the grade you teach?

- What support do you need for your teaching this year? What supports exist in your school?

- Read this article that details using <u>Universal Design for Learning to design assessments</u> and discuss or write down reactions. See **https://tinyurl.com/ UDLtipsAssessments**.

General Recommendations

Key ideas

- Engage parents in the assessment process early and often. Have flexible ways for parents and caregivers to be able to share insights about students' strengths and areas where they may have concerns.

- Keep assessments short. They should be comprised of informal quick checks and authentic moments you can use to assess the skills you are working on.

- Design assessments to focus on what students can do instead of focusing on deficits. By doing so, we can help students develop a growth mindset about education.

Discussion questions

- Share two assessments that you already use to informally check students' skills related to reading, math, or other.

  Sentence starter:
  - An assessment I already use to informally check in on student learning is . . .

- Can you think of a third formative assessment that might help you understand what students can do?

  Sentence starter:
  - To better understand students' strengths, I could . . .

Have more time or want to learn more?

- How can you engage parents and caregivers in the assessment process early and often?

- List three short assessments you could design or modify that would demonstrate what students know or can do.

Assessment Examples

Key ideas

- **Example #1:** Identify thinking habits or routines that students can develop and practice in reading, math, and other subjects (such as the nonfiction reading example from the video). In the video, we saw stations become a formative assessment opportunity.

- **Example #2:** Allow students to choose a goal they want to work on. Identify what success looks like and give students flexible opportunities to work toward those goals.

- **Example #3:** Include opportunities for students to choose what they read or try related to the learning goal.

- **Example #4:** Allow students to make and share videos that demonstrate what they have learned. Reflect on the learning process with students and caregivers throughout the year to build the growth mindset. Frame assessment and learning as a process of continuous growth with parents and caregivers; for example, you can do this in a letter you send home.

- **Example #5:** Use sentence starters to help students share and communicate in a productive way about their learning process (such as the popsicle-stick examples from the video).

Discussion questions

- Share one of the assessment strategies from the video that you would like to use or that you already use in your classroom.

  Sentence starter:

  ○ An assessment strategy I could use from the video is . . .

- How can you help students create their own learning goals?

  Sentence starter:

  ○ To help students create their own learning goals, I can . . .

Have more time or want to learn more?

- Take time to write your first letter home to parents explaining your approach to assessment. Or create a list of 5 to 10 bullets to remind you of items to include in the letter you write later.

- How do you approach the "I cannot do this yet" approach to learning and the growth mindset?

- How could you use some version of the popsicle-stick example to encourage students to share their learning process with each other?

Conclusion

Key ideas

- Choose one idea to try out in your classroom, such as focusing on formative assessments for the first few months of the year.
- Evaluate the quality of one of your assessments using the suggestions in this video.
- Approach this year as the "year of growth mindset" to embrace the power of the learning process.

Discussion questions

- How will you gather formative feedback at the start of this school year?
- What are the next steps you will take to evaluate your assessments?

Resources for Grades K–2

- An article from *Edutopia* on "Why Ages 2–7 Matter So Much for Brain Development" is available at **https://tinyurl.com/Edutopia2-7**.
- Scholastic provides some creative formative assessment ideas for young children at **https://tinyurl .com/ScholasticFormative/**.
- A video on fun math and movement to get young learners excited and engaged is at **https://www .youtube.com/watch?v=1dkPouLWCyc**.

Check out the full list of resources at the end of the playbook, including strategies to connect with parents and families.

Assessments for Grades 3–5

Welcome and Introduction

"Assessments for Grades 3–5" video (See **https:// tinyurl.com/CASTvideo3-5**.)

In grades 3–5, students may be comfortable with the routines and habits of schools and are building on foundational reading comprehension and decoding skills as well as math skills. They are also shifting from learning to read to reading to learn. In addition, more socialization and project-oriented learning is taking place. This is when students first experience larger standardized tests. In this video, we share specific barriers related to this age group, as well as general recommendations, tips, and strategies.

General Recommendations

Key ideas

- Conduct assessments that isolate school-related skills from content-related or academic skills.

- Create assessments that allow students to show what they know using video. Video can be used throughout the year as a way for students to reflect on their growth and learning over time.

- Embed reflection time into assessments so students can develop a better understanding of how they learn.

Discussion questions

- What are you most worried about as you return to school this year?

  Sentence starter:

  ○ A concern I have as we return to school this year is . . .

Have more time or want to learn more?

- What are some of the key skills students need to learn? What are some of the core content pieces they need to learn? How are these different from some of the school-related skills?

- What are some ways you support the growth mindset with your students?

- In what ways can you use video to support student learning?

- What do you need as a teacher to support you in your work this year?

- Find tips using <u>Universal Design for Learning to design assessments</u> and discuss or make note of ideas. See **https://tinyurl.com/UDLtipsAssessments**.

Assessment Examples

Key ideas

- **Example #1:** Review your assessments for confusing questions, built-in biases, and assumptions about background experiences.

- **Example #2:** Try assessments more than once and at different times of the day.

- **Example #3:** Have flexible resources reliably available in the learning environment so students can get used to using those resources.

- **Example #4:** Focus on mastery-oriented feedback including sharing strategies to build specific areas for growth.

- **Example #5:** Try to engage with parents and caregivers early in the year and keep them in the loop.

Consider sending a letter home to gain information from parents and caregivers about their child.

- **Example #6:** Incorporate growth mindset into your assessments. For example, encourage students to identify the kinds of mistakes they made and what they may do to take next steps to learn. Or have students make a video to narrate their process as they work. These videos can help teachers identify where students may be struggling and what their strengths are. Videos can show improvement over time, an important aspect of growth mindset.

- **Example #7:** Help students learn how to take tests and teach students how to use the different tools available in standardized tests.

- **Example #8:** Incorporate real-world examples in your assessments to make them relevant and engaging.

- **Example #9:** Create open-writing prompts to learn more about students and their social-emotional learning, as well as their writing skills.

Discussion questions

- In what ways can you use video to support your learning goals in your classroom?

  Sentence starter:

  ○ I could use video by . . .

- List three assessment ideas you can incorporate into your classroom.

  Sentence starter:

  ○ Three ideas for assessments include . . .

Have more time or want to learn more?

- How can you embed the concept of the growth mind-set into your assessments?
- How can you engage parents in the assessment process early and often?
- How can you teach students about test-taking skills and available tools?
- How can you include video as a way to highlight a growth mindset?
- In what ways can you use open-writing prompts to learn more about students' interests? What are other ways students can respond to the prompts, such as with text-to-speech or voice recording?

Conclusion

Key ideas

- Focus on giving formative assessments early in the school year.
- Evaluate the quality of the assessments you use.
- Commit to making this school year the "year of growth mindset."

Discussion questions

- How might you create an assessment that includes students' advice to themselves, as described in the video?

  Sentence starter:
  - I could create an opportunity for students to give advice to themselves by . . .

- How can you evaluate the quality of your assessments using tips from this video?

  Sentence starter:

  ○ To increase the relevance of my assessments, I can . . .

Have more time or want to learn more?

- Take time to write your first letter home to parents explaining your approach to assessment. Or write a list of 5 to 10 bullets that will remind you of items to include in the letter.

- What are some ways you can incorporate relevant experiences for students into some of your assessments? What should you be careful of if you decide to take this approach?

- What barriers might students experience in the assessment or learning experience?

- Read this article and share which of the seven tips you think is most critical or which you plan to incorporate into your classroom. See **https://tinyurl.com/7tipsAnxiety**.

Resources for Grades 3–5

- Read CAST's "UDL Tips for Assessments" at **https://tinyurl.com/UDLtipsAssessments**.

Check out the full list of resources at the end of the playbook, including strategies for connecting with parents and families.

Assessments for Grades 6–8

Welcome and Introduction

"Assessments for Grades 6–8" video (See **https://tinyurl.com/CASTvideo6-8**.)

In grades 6–8, students are well acclimated to school and are becoming much more independent and cued into the social aspects of school. In this video, we share specific barriers related to this age group, general recommendations, and tips and strategies.

Key ideas

- With online and remote learning, students have been communicating more in virtual spaces.
- Relationships and mental health issues (such as stress and anxiety) may start to manifest more at this age.

Discussion questions

- What are you most worried about as you return to school this year?

  Sentence starter:

  ○ This year, I am concerned about . . .

- In what ways could you use support in your work this year?

- Read "UDL Tips for Assessments" at **https://tinyurl.com/UDLtipsAssessments**. Discuss or make a note of reactions.

General Recommendations

Key ideas

- Codesign assessments with learners. At this age, students want more voice and control over their learning, and we can do this by getting student input in our assessments and lessons.

- Keep assessments relevant; for example, include students' interests and real-world examples or experiences.

- Build technology skills to provide flexible options for assessment and for collaboration. Support students to use the technology; this works whether we are teaching in the classroom or remotely.

Discussion questions

- List a few strategies you could use in the upcoming year that would allow students to codesign assessments with you.

  Sentence starter:

  - To encourage students to codesign assessments, I can . . .

- How can you integrate assessments that specifically focus on ensuring that students can use technology tools to support them to do their best on the assessment (for example, consider speech-to-text, verbal responses, and the use of diagrams or images)?

  Sentence starter:

  - Technology tools students can use on assessments include . . .

Have more time or want to learn more?

- In what ways can you make assessments more relevant for your students?

- How can different technology strategies work in different contexts, such as remote, hybrid, or face to face?

- How can you encourage parents and caregivers to communicate with you as needed, around both the assessment process and learning?

Assessment Examples

Key ideas

- **Example #1:** Increase autonomy and space for students to decide what steps to take or where they need to go for help. For example, ask students to make their own test questions or consider integrating student self-report notes.

- **Example #2:** At the beginning of the year, keep assessments short, informal, and targeted. Focus assessments on specific areas or skills and let students know the goal and purpose of these assessments.

- **Example #3:** Support students in the social and emotional roles they need to learn to collaborate. Practice working in groups online and in person.

- **Example #4:** Teach students how to use technology supports and options that may be helpful for their learning.

- **Example #5:** Communicate with families and caregivers about their children as learners, including their strengths.

- Remember, some students will do better in remote learning settings.
- Support students' executive functions by highlighting the different scaffolds and tools they can use. For example, ask students which learning strategies they used to prepare for an assessment, or encourage different students to be note-takers. Note-taking is a specific skill that can be taught, modeled, and scaffolded, and there are many ways students can take notes. Notes can be a formative assessment.

Discussion questions

- How can you encourage students to create their own test questions using the learning goals for that assessment?

  Sentence starter:

  - To encourage students to create their own test questions, I can . . .

- Reflect on the student self-report notes discussed in the video. How can you incorporate this idea into your classroom?

  Sentence starter:

  - Self-report notes could be used by . . .

Have more time or want to learn more?

- How do you support students to learn more about what they need to succeed in assessments?
- What are some ways you can make your assessments more relevant to students? What should you be careful of if you decide to take this approach?
- How can you teach and assess collaborative skills, whether in face-to-face, hybrid, or remote settings?

- Think of two summative assessments you typically give at the beginning of the school year. Use these three key questions to evaluate the quality of each. What can you change about each assessment to improve it?

  - How is the assessment aligned to the learning goals?

  - How does the assessment engage the learner?

  - What barriers might students experience with this assessment?

- How can you support note-taking sharing and strategies? Brainstorm ways you can use student notes, or other tools, to conduct formative assessments.

- Take time to craft your first letter home to parents that explains your approach to assessment. Or write a list of 5 to 10 bullets that will remind you of items to include in the letter.

Conclusion

Key ideas

- Focus on giving formative assessments early in the school year.

- Evaluate the quality of the assessments you use.

- Commit to making this school year the "year of growth mindset," a fundamental belief that embraces the power of learning.

Discussion questions

- How will you plan to give formative assessments at the start of the year?

- How will you evaluate the quality of the assessments you use?

Resources for Grades 6-8

- See this module on <u>using UDL to plan instruction</u> that supports all students at the middle school level at **https://tinyurl.com/IRISmoduleUDL**.

- Watch this <u>video on mini whiteboards</u> (**https://tinyurl.com/MiniWhiteBoardVideo**). There's also a good <u>blog post</u> on the topic at **https://tinyurl.com/MiniWhiteBoardBlog**. And download this <u>research paper</u> on the impact that using mini whiteboards has on increasing older students' engagement at **https://tinyurl.com/MiniWhiteBoardResearch**.

- Read <u>"UDL Tips for Assessments"</u> at **https://tinyurl.com/UDLtipsAssessments**. Discuss or make notes about reactions.

Check out the full list of resources at the end of the playbook, including strategies to connect with parents and families.

Assessments for Grades 9-12

Welcome and Introduction

<u>"Assessments for Grades 9–12" video</u> (See **https://tinyurl.com/CASTvideo9-12**.)

In grades 9–12, students are more independent in their learning and have had years of experiences in school—and students in this age group may have developed more of a sense of what they think they can and cannot do well. In this video, we share specific barriers related to this age group, general recommendations, and tips and strategies.

Key ideas

- Think about equity and recognize the differences in access, background, and opportunity for practice.
- SATs and other large-scale assessments are important at this age.
- During the COVID quarantine, students likely spent more time than usual in isolation and on their devices. Disparities due to the pandemic may persist.

Discussion questions

- What are you most worried about as you return to school this year?

  Sentence starter:
  - I am most concerned about . . .
- In what ways could you use support in your work this year?
- Read the "UDL Tips for Assessments" at **https://tinyurl.com/UDLtipsAssessments**. Discuss or note your reactions.

General Recommendations

Key ideas

- Use preassessments to engage students in the learning process and habits of learning. Make connections to what students already know and can do.
- Create assessments that give students the opportunity to transfer skills. Make assessments authentic to real-world examples so they can transfer the skills to careers.

- Focus on giving mastery-oriented feedback. Use assessments to engage students in reflection to deepen their understanding of their own learning.

Discussion questions

- How often do you use preassessments to engage students? Could you use them more frequently? How?

  Sentence starter:

  ○ I use preassessments . . . and could also try . . .

- How do you assess whether a student can transfer what they have learned into another context or situation?

  Sentence starter:

  ○ To assess how well students can transfer what they have learned into a new situation, I . . .

Have more time or want to learn more?

- In what ways can you include relevant examples from the real world in your assessments?

- How can you reflect with students about their learning and assessment?

- How can you engage parents in the assessment process early and often?

- List a few strategies you could use in the upcoming year that would allow students to codesign assessments with you and make them more relevant.

- Explain what mastery-oriented feedback is in your own words. How often are you incorporating mastery-oriented feedback into the preparation for and actual assessments?

Assessment Examples

Key ideas

- **Example #1:** The goal of preassessments is to help us uncover connections we can make for students and to peak students' interest in the upcoming topics.

- **Example #2:** Use preassessments to help students explore the boundaries of their understanding, which helps them set their own learning goals.

- **Example #3:** Avoid high-risk assessments. Instead, focus on preassessments that are not high risk and can lower stress about assessments. Increase the weight of formative assessments.

- **Example #4:** Focus on relevance in assessments: show, don't tell. Consider how students can show what they know in different formats, in games, and in different situational contexts. Increase the connection between knowledge and action.

- **Example #5:** Recognize the importance of authentic formative assessments that measure not only what students know but also what they can do.

- **Example #6:** Use a letter home to gain information about students' strengths and challenges—and include students in those conversations.

- **Example #7:** Use assessments as an opportunity for you and your students to engage in dialogue about their learning. Focus on and communicate about the growth mindset. Give feedback that is specific and that encourages the learner to reengage with the assessment and work toward providing their own solution.

Discussion questions

- How do you currently weigh formative vs. summative assessments in the overall design of your class? What would happen if you shifted the value to increase the weight of formative assessments?

  Sentence starter:

  ○ If I weigh formative assessments more, this would . . .

- How can you incorporate a growth mindset into your classroom and into assessments? Why is doing so especially important this year?

  Sentence starter:

  ○ A way to incorporate the growth mindset into my classroom this year is to . . .

Have more time or want to learn more?

- Think of two formative assessments you typically give at the beginning of the school year. Use these three key questions to evaluate the quality of each.

  ○ How is the assessment linked to the learning goals?

  ○ How does the assessment engage the learner?

  ○ What barriers might students experience?

- What are some ways in which you could make your assessments more relevant?

- How can you make time to meet with students one on one, whether for in-person, hybrid, or remote environments?

- Take time to craft your first letter home to parents explaining your approach to assessment. Or write a list of 5 to 10 bullets that will remind you of things to include in the letter later.

Conclusion

Key ideas

- Focus on giving formative assessments early in the school year.
- Evaluate the quality of the assessments you use.
- Commit to making this school year the "year of growth mindset"—a fundamental belief that embraces the power of learning.

Discussion questions

- How will you plan to give formative assessments at the start of the year?
- How will you evaluate the quality of the assessments you use?

Resources for Grades 9–12

- The research paper "Acting, Knowing, Learning, Simulating, Gaming" shows the importance of helping students *show*, not just *tell*, what they know. See **https://tinyurl.com/Crookall**.

- Watch this video on mini whiteboards (**https://tinyurl.com/MiniWhiteBoardVideo**). There's also a good blog post on the topic at **https://tinyurl.com/MiniWhiteBoardBlog**. And download this research paper on the impact that using mini whiteboards has on increasing the engagement of older students at **https://tinyurl.com/MiniWhiteBoardResearch**.

- Read Grant Wiggins's "Seven Keys to Effective Feedback" at **https://tinyurl.com/Wiggins7**.

- See what the UDL Guidelines have to say about the <u>UDL approach to mastery-oriented feedback</u> at **https://tinyurl.com/GuidelinesMastery**.

- Lexia Learning offers <u>six tips to help students develop a growth mindset</u> at **https://www.tinyurl .com/Lexia6tips**.

- See this <u>article that details using UDL tips for assessments</u> at **https://tinyurl.com/UDLtipsAssessments**.

- Check out the full list of resources at the end of the playbook, including strategies to connect with parents and families.

Section 2

Resources for Educators

Learn More About UDL

Websites

- Learn more about CAST's work at **https://www.cast.org**.

- Take a deep dive into CAST's UDL Guidelines for strategies to reduce barriers at **https://udlguidelines.cast.org**.

- UDL On Campus has concrete strategies for assessments at **http://udloncampus.cast.org/page/assessment_udl**.

- Get certified in Universal Design for Learning (UDL) at **https://learningdesigned.org/content/credentials**. For states, districts, or schools interested in learning more about the certification opportunities and packages for educators, please email us at **info@learningdesigned.org**.

Articles

- "UDL: A Teacher's Guide" by Allison Posey, one of the authors of this publication, is available at **https://tinyurl.com/UDLteacherGuide**.

- See Allison Posey's ideas for lesson planning with UDL at **https://tinyurl.com/UDLlessonplan**.

- Explore the Learning Designed platform to find UDL resources, credentials, and networking opportunities at **https://learningdesigned.org**.

- Understand how Universal Design for Learning supports the learning brain. See **https://tinyurl.com/UDLNeuro**.

- Read and discuss "UDL Tips for Assessments." See **https://tinyurl.com/UDLtipsAssessments**.

Videos or webinars

- See research scientist Samantha Daley's take on UDL, variability, and emotion in learning at **https://tinyurl.com/DaleyUDL**.

Books

- Universal Design for Learning: Theory and Practice lays out the foundations of UDL. You can see the full version online at **https://udltheorypractice.cast.org**.

- See dozens of books and resources on UDL and accessibility at **http://castpublishing.org**.

Learn More About Accessibility

- Five Things Educators Can Do to Buy Accessible
- Designing for Accessibility with POUR

- Vetting for Accessibility
- Creating Accessible Documents
- Creating Accessible Video
- Creating Accessible Social Media Posts

Videos or webinars

- What Is Accessibility?
- Creating and Curating Accessible OER with Confidence

Learn More About Assessments

Websites

- *Edutopia* suggests 7 Smart, Fast Ways to Do Formative Assessments. See **https://tinyurl.com /Edutopia7**.
- ASCD offers a study guide on formative assessments (recommended books, articles, etc.). See **https:// tinyurl.com/ASCDformAssess**.
- Read Jana Nicol's piece on putting learning goals front and center where all students can access them. See **https://www.theudlproject.com/blog /goal-setting**.
- CAST offers "UDL Tips for Assessments." See **https:// tinyurl.com/UDLtipsAssessments**.

Articles

- TIES Center and CAST distance learning teamed up for a piece on using data to inform instruction. See **https://tinyurl.com/TIESdataCollection**.
- "UDL and Assessment." See **http://udloncampus .cast.org/page/assessment_udl**.

- Accurate and Informative for All: Universal Design for Learning (UDL) and the Future of Assessment is a brief by researchers at CAST that is published in the *Handbook of Accessible Instruction and Testing Practices* (Springer, 2016, 167–180).

Books

- *Using Formative Assessment to Improve Student Outcomes in Classrooms,* by Michael Connell (CAST, 2019). See **http://castpublishing.org** for more information.

Learn More About Engagement

Websites

- Use the RULER and mood meter from Yale Center for Emotional Intelligence to help students learn to assess emotions and to discuss how emotions can be a barrier or helpful to learning. See **https://www.ycei .org/ruler**. Watch a short video on the mood meter (see **https://tinyurl.com/MoodMeterVideo**) or look at how Seattle Public Schools use it (**https://tinyurl. com/SeattleMoodMeter**).

- See CAST's UDL On Campus on Emotion and Learning at **http://udloncampus.cast.org/page /teach_emotion**.

- Check out CAST's UDL On Campus page on Social Learning. See **http://udloncampus.cast.org/page /teach_social**.

- The National AEM Center at CAST offers ideas on how to personalize the reading experience. See **https:/tinyurl.com/AEMpersonalizedReading**.

- CAST offers UDL tips for designing an engaging learning environment. See **https://tinyurl.com /CASTtipsEngage**.
- Vanderbilt's Center for Teaching suggests ways to design PowerPoint presentations that better engage students. See **https://tinyurl.com/BetterPowerPt**.
- Yale Center for Emotional Intelligence has research and classroom examples on integrating emotions into learning. See **https://www.ycei.org/**.

Articles

- "We Feel, Therefore We Learn" by Mary Helen Immordino-Yang explores the central role of emotion for learning. Download for free at **https://tinyurl .com/ScienceSocialEmotion2**.
- Allison Posey details how to support the emotional link to learning, including how to use UDL and the Yale Mood Meter to support students' emotions, at **https://tinyurl.com/PoseyEmotion**.
- The TIES Center also writes on how to understand and communicate about emotions for deeper learning. See **https://tinyurl.com/TIESemotion**.

Video

- Watch "We Feel, Therefore We Learn: The Neuroscience of Social Emotion" by Dr. Mary Helen Immordino-Yang of the University of Southern California. See **https://tinyurl.com/ScienceSocialEmotion**.

Books

- *Permission to Feel: Unlocking the Power of Emotions to Help Our Kids, Ourselves, and Our Society Thrive* (Celadon/Macmillan, 2019) by Marc Brackett, founder and director of the Yale Center for Emotional Intelligence.

- *Engage the Brain: How to Design for Learning That Taps into the Power of Emotions* (ASCD, 2018) by CAST's Allison Posey, one of the authors of this guide.

Learn More About Connecting with Parents and Families

Websites

- Understood.com has a set of helpful articles about engaging with families and caregivers; the articles include ideas on how to improve communication, have difficult conversations, and partner together. See **https://tinyurl.com/PartnerFamiliesUnderstood**.

- For communicating about autism, check out the article "Decreasing Fears and Stresses Through Parent-Professional Partnerships" by Gray, Msall, & Msall that appeared in *Infants & Young Children, 21*(4), 256–271.

- See the article "Gathering and Giving Information With Families" by Woods & Lindeman that appeared in *Infants & Young Children, 21*(4), 272–284.

Suggestions

- Strategies
  - Offer flexible ways for parents and caregivers to be in touch with you.
  - Move from an interview to a conversation. Don't just ask questions, provide space for parents and caregivers to ask questions as well.

- Start with student strengths and what is going well with the student.

- Ask parents and caregivers to problem solve with you. Ask about routines, the learning environment, family interests, strategies for transitioning, and goals.

- If a caregiver is reluctant to answer a question, offer friendly but specific questions based on observations you have made in the classroom or based on classroom goals.

- Offer a strategy that has worked well in the past and explain why it worked.

- Explain why this information is important and how you plan to use it.

- Reiterate the goal in order to work together to support the learner.

Connecting with Parents and Caregivers

Understood.com offers tips on how to write an effective email to parents and caregivers. See https://tinyurl.com/EmailCaregivers. The following Letter Home Ideas could be included in a letter to parents and caregivers at the start of the school year:

- What is your preferred method of communication (text, email, phone call, etc.)?
- What is the best time to reach out to you?
- What are the strengths of your child?
    - Academic . . .
    - Character . . .
    - Physical . . .

- What are you concerned about for this upcoming year?
  - Has your child seemed disengaged from school during remote learning?
  - Has your child enjoyed learning online or in a remote setting more? Why?
- What has worked well in the past for your child at home or in school?
  - Does your child enjoy working in groups or as part of a team?
  - Have you talked with your child about the ways/ environments that help them learn?
- What kind of teacher do you need me to be for your child?
  - What systems have you noticed that leave your child feeling successful?
  - When your child is struggling, what are the best ways to keep them motivated?

Considerations for sharing with and asking of parents and caregivers:

- Consider sharing a "live," updateable version of your syllabus that includes links to folders and calendars so parents can help students and see upcoming assignments/deadlines. See https://tinyurl.com /syllabusplan.
- Consider asking: When (what time of day) does your child seem most interested in learning?

About the Editors

<u>Amanda Bastoni</u> is an Education Research Scientist at CAST. Before joining CAST in 2019, Amanda was a Career and Technical Education (CTE) director and teacher with 20+ years of experience in K–12 educational leadership, journalism, and business. She has developed new pathways and programs targeted to meet the needs of English language learners and nontraditional students, created interdisciplinary courses, organized fundraising campaigns, developed educational publicity programs, and written educational articles for local and national outlets. Specifically, she has sought to use UDL to increase pathways for English language learners and females interested in exploring STEM careers.

Amanda was named New Hampshire's 2019 CTE Leader of the Year. She is the coauthor of two books: *From the Inside-Out: Concrete Steps to Transforming Education Today* (Rowman and Littlefield, 2020) and *Making Room for Change: Finding Ways to Leverage Time to Benefit All Students* (Rowman and Littlefield, 2021). She holds a doctorate in education from New England College.

Allison Posey, Senior Content Editor and Producer at CAST, leads the development of materials that support the design of learning experiences to reach and engage neurodiverse learners. She also leads professional development programs and opportunities that integrate current understandings from brain science with effective instructional practices. She hosts the CAST free webinar series and is the author of *Engage the Brain: How to Design for Learning That Taps into the Power of Emotion* (ASCD, 2018) and the coauthor with Katie Novak of *Unlearning: Changing Your Beliefs and Your Classroom with UDL* (CAST, 2020).

Prior to coming to CAST, Allison was a life science teacher in high school and community college settings; she taught courses such as genetics, anatomy, physiology, biology, neuroscience, and psychology. She received a master's degree in Mind, Brain, and Education from Harvard Graduate School of Education where she also worked as a teaching fellow for courses such as Educational Neuroscience and Framing Scientific Research for Public Understanding.

CPSIA information can be obtained
at www.ICGtesting.com
Printed in the USA
BVHW050552140721
611605BV00006B/75

9 781930 583771